Elba Island, Italy Coloring Book

By: Jobe Leonard

Elba Island, Italy Coloring Book

www.Jobe.ws

Copyright © Jobe Leonard 2014

This book is sold subject to the condition that it shall not, by way of trade or otherwise, be lent, resold, hired out, or otherwise circulated without the publisher's prior consent in any form of binding or cover other than that in which it is published and without a similar condition, being imposed on the subsequent publisher.

For information about special discounts, bulk purchases, or autographed editions please contact Jobe Leonard at
JobeLeonard@gmail.com

Write to:

Jobe Leonard Books

1511 Mayflower Lane

Dandridge, TN 37725

Or visit:

www.Jobe.ws

Copyright © 2014 Jobe Leonard

All rights reserved.

**ISBN-13:
978-1503075894**

**ISBN-10:
1503075893**

CONTENTS

Street	4
Beach	5
Coast	6
Thicket	7
Rocks	8
Island	9
Valley	10
Hill	11
Glory	12
Cliff	13
Clouds	14
Signs	15
Fort	16
Exile	17
Napoleon	18
Sky	19
Stairs	20
Ferry	21
Port	22
Bay	23
About the author	24

Elba Island, Italy Coloring Book

www.Jobe.ws

Street

Beach

Elba Island, Italy Coloring Book

www.Jobe.ws

Coast

Thicket

Elba Island, Italy Coloring Book

www.Jobe.ws

Rocks

Island

Elba Island, Italy Coloring Book

www.Jobe.ws

Valley

Hill

Elba Island, Italy Coloring Book

www.Jobe.ws

Glory

Cliff

Elba Island, Italy Coloring Book

www.Jobe.ws

Clouds

Signs

Elba Island, Italy Coloring Book

www.Jobe.ws

Fort

Exile

Elba Island, Italy Coloring Book

www.Jobe.ws

Napoleon

Sky

Elba Island, Italy Coloring Book

www.Jobe.ws

Stairs

Ferry

Elba Island, Italy Coloring Book

www.Jobe.ws

Port

Bay

About the Author

Jobe Leonard lives in Dandridge, TN. After attending Tennessee Technological University, he received his MBA at Lincoln Memorial University. He has over 20 titles published on travel, construction, and architecture. He is a project manager with Hearthstone Homes and has currently built over 150 custom log and timber homes in 30 different states. This includes a recent project he managed that was named the 2012 National Log Home of the Year. For more information on his current projects, visit www.Jobe.ws.

If you enjoyed reading this guide I would appreciate your honest review on Amazon, Facebook, or Twitter. Also tell a friend and help me spread the word. Send any questions to JobeLeonard@gmail.com

Printed in Dunstable, United Kingdom